yourself enough to be healthy

50 Affirmations to your best life

By
Basheerah Ahmad, MS, CPT, MHR

ISBN:1-4635-7603-X
ISBN-13:978-1-4635-7603-5

DEDICATION

This book is dedicated to my phenomenal family; who never questions my ambition, never doubts my abilities, and who continuously reminds me to follow my God-given Destiny.

"Mom, Dad, Aquilah, Iman, Jihan, Hana, Ahmad, and Ma'isah- I love you".

AUTHOR'S NOTE...

Almost on a daily basis, I run into people who tell me that *"Love yourself enough to be Healthy"* is such a smart slogan or that it's a great branding idea. Little do they realize that this statement is so much more than a slogan, it's the philosophy that I adopted on life to save me from MY self-sabotaging ways.

Most people who know or who have met Basheerah Ahmad would say that she is happy, sweet, and optimistic. And while these characteristics do apply to me, they certainly do not sum up the complexities that define me. So often, people assume that the perpetual smile on my face means that I don't have the same adversities that everyone else does; or that I have a secret solution to success in life. Nothing could be further from my truth...I've had more bumps in my journey, than many of you would ever believe.

You see, I was a privileged child and teenager; not in a financial sense, but in a mentally and physically protected way. I grew up in a home filled with Love, Knowledge, Ambition, Spirituality, and sense of Community Responsibility. I was raised to believe that every human being was "good" on the inside. In fact, I'll never forget one of the many lessons that my parents taught me about sharing. I have 3 wonderful sisters, Aquilah, Iman, and Jihan, and on all of our birthdays, my parents would have us use our allowance money to throw a party for our friends in the neighborhood. My mother and father felt that the best way for us to celebrate our day of creation, was to give something back to Humanity.

Another memory I have of giving back still stings a little, but I honor my father for the lesson. When my older sister and I were no more than 4 and 6 years old, my father took us to **Toys R' Us** to pick out toys and games. We were so excited and felt on top of the world! Mom and Dad were very careful with their spending, so a shopping spree for toys was almost unheard of. Little did we know (or didn't care to remember) that all of the toys were being purchased to give to the children at a nearby inner city childcare center. Needless to say, my sister and I were devastated. We were too young to understand that the toys we thought were "so cool" were probably the only toys that these children would see at all.

Some of you may consider that insensitive behavior on my father's part, and I must admit that I was pretty upset for years. But, my father and mother taught us how to serve God's people before serving ourselves, and this message is still deeply embroidered into the fabric that I am today. Unfortunately, we live in a world of people who have been so damaged and desensitized, that they prey on individuals who live by this pure system of service.

At times I'm embarrassed to admit that I became one of these individuals who people tried to prey on. Even with all of the academic knowledge and social consciousness that I possessed, I became a target. As I grew into an adult and begin to spread my wings outside the comfort and protection of my parents' home, I was hit with a startling realization. Yes, it's true that everyone may have the potential to be a good person, but many have given up on even trying to.

It was at this point in my life that I began to feel bitter, and question if something was wrong with my view on creation. Why did I always try to see the best side of people even when they didn't even want to acknowledge it for themselves? I started to turn inward and pulled myself away from society because I didn't understand how people could be so cruel to each other. I didn't comprehend why people could throw their lives away. I'm embarrassed to admit that at one point, I wouldn't even return the phone calls from friends or family for weeks at a time. I didn't want to save anyone anymore, including myself.

These were very dark days for me, and until now, only my older sister Aquilah knew about them. Yes, little Miss High Achiever went through a period of Depression, that she hid from the people most important in her life. But, of course I was in denial about my Depression, so I refused to talk about it, and slowly it began to change me. For the first time in my life, I allowed fear to creep in and affect my decision-making. I started thinking of myself as a statistic. "Why was I in my early thirties and not married? Why didn't I have kids? Why didn't I work a 9-to-5 in Corporate America? Why didn't I have solid investments and an American Express Card? Surely there had to be something wrong with me, or people wouldn't keep asking me these questions. Right?" Yes, I had "Drank the Kool-Aid".

The Basheerah Ahmad from just a few years previously would never have allowed these asinine societal pressures to take a moment of her time! The old me knew without question that she was created from the Best of Molds, and could accomplish any goal she set her heart and mind to. I began to pay closer attention to the people that I would have around me, and I started to see that what was happening to me, was also happening to many of my close friends. We were questioning our

Greatness because we were looking at our lives in Worldly timetables.

When I started to clearly see myself and my "sick" thinking pattern through the eyes of others, I realized that I had to snap out of this depressed state before it caused serious damage to my self-esteem. At this point in my life, I started listening to affirmations. My favorite Self-Help Author is Louise Hay. I would force myself to repeat her affirmations over and over, until they became imbedded in my memory bank, and it worked! Whenever I began to have a negative, self-destructive thought, my newly trained subconscious brain would come to the rescue and silence my overactive conscious mind. I began to re-build my confidence, determination, and will to help others again. I was ready to "Love myself enough to be healthy".

This statement has different meanings for different people. For me it means, having a love affair with myself that is so solid and genuine that I can't hurt myself in any way without immediately feeling guilty. Now,

I know my VALUE - and with this book, I challenge you to find and know yours.

It brings tears to my eyes to think of the phenomenal men and women in this world, who give up on their dreams and ambitions, because they never learned how to put self-love first. Think about it. If every elementary program in this country alone started each day out with an "I am worthy of Love" Mantra, imagine how high children from all racial and socio-economic backgrounds could hold their heads. I wonder how many young girls would save their Virginity for a deserving mate instead of feeling obligated to serve the first Man that makes them feel special.

My mother and father were certainly on the right track by teaching me to serve and love others, but as I've grown into this woman today, I've taken their message a step further and learned how to love me. Every affirmation in this book comes from my heart and has helped me in overcoming adversity. I ask that you read each one carefully and repeat it daily until your heart accepts its truth.

I pray that these affirmations change your life as they have changed mine. I implore you to be Freedom, be Peace, and most of all, be Love.

My heart is with yours,

Basheerah Ahmad

Love Yourself Enough to Be Healthy: 50 Affirmations to Your Best Life

By Basheerah Ahmad, MS, CPT, MHR

FOREWORD

One of the most highly discussed topics in our lives today is the declining state of our health. Everywhere you turn, there are commercials, infomercials, articles, books, and plenty of television shows, all promising to give you what you need to look and feel your best. But what many of these numerous media portals fail to do is to tie health back to its original source, the spirit. A healthy body simply cannot be achieved in the absence of a healthy spirit.

So how do we attain this healthy spirit? A more appropriate question would be, "How do we re-create this healthy spirit?" When we entered this life, we came as innocent harmonious creatures who neither judged others nor ourselves. Our minds, bodies, and spirits were clean slates. But, as we developed and became indoctrinated to our surroundings, we also became aware of our inequities and perceived shortcomings. This awareness served as opposition to our natural growth potential. We then became beings that exhibited envy, excessive ambition, prejudice, and worst of all, self-hate; thus, we became incongruent with our natural constitution.

This disconnect with our spirit wasn't just on a mental/emotional level, but it also occurred on the physical level. When our bodies are out of sync with their inherited nature, pain and illness begin to manifest in many ways, which often include disease and/or depression.

So how do we begin to reconnect to our natural beginnings, or to our spirit? How do we get back on track to becoming the human beings that we were meant to be? This process must begin by focusing on our minds and spirits. Healthy eating and consistent exercise are wonderful catalysts in obtaining long-term health, but they are just pieces of the entire puzzle.

It fascinates me to see so many people justify the separation of mental, physical, and spiritual health. I often see scholars and professionals who have reached the pinnacle of educational success, yet they are riddled with negative thoughts, habits, and in many cases, actual physical disease. For reasons that are logical to them, their intellectual health takes precedence over their physical and emotional health.

One of the simplest ways to bring your mind and body back in sync with your spirit is through repeating positive affirmations. We are what we believe we are, and affirmations are a powerful tool to reprogram our thinking. The repeated words help to focus the mind on its objective. By using the conscious mind to replay the positive affirmation, the subconscious also begins to adopt the intended message. A healthy subconscious mind will ultimately lead to a healthier existence.

Imagine waking every morning with only love for self and others in your heart. What an amazing world we would live in if every human being operated from a position of love. I've been accused of being an optimist, but I truly believe that in time (maybe not my lifetime) our world can recover from its destructive, chaotic, and demonic practices, and become what it was intended to be.

The affirmations in this book were all created to be a constant reminder to you of your inherent potential to be great. Please read them daily and let them resonate in your mind. You can learn to "Love yourself enough to be healthy."

AFFIRMATIONS

I.

I choose to live my very best life.

We do ourselves a huge disservice by believing that health is primarily about being a certain weight or size. True health can only be achieved once you recognize that you are worthy of love. Healthy living is a choice.

"If you don't run your own life, somebody else will."

~ John Atkins

II.

I will forgive everyone in my life, past or present, who has caused me harm.

Harboring resentment and pain can cause the manifestation of illness within you. Forgiveness is one of the most precious gifts that you can give to yourself.

"When you hold resentment toward another, you are bound to that person or condition by an emotional link that is stronger than steel. Forgiveness is the only way to dissolve that link and get free."

~ Catherine Ponder

III.

I am comfortable in my own skin.

Society will consistently try to sell you the lie that you're not pretty enough, thin enough, or smart enough, but there comes a point in your life when you have to say, "Enough is enough. I love me, for me."

"If I were you, I would stand for something—I would count!"

~ Benjamin E. Mays

IV.

*I will only work toward
becoming the best I can be.*

You were created to be the very best; therefore, only expect greatness from yourself. Many of us waste valuable time questioning our natural abilities. What are you waiting for? Time waits for no man or woman.

"You were not born a winner, and you were not born a loser. You are what you make yourself be."

~ Lou Holtz

V.

My family will learn to live healthy by watching consistent examples from me.

As you embark on your health journey, people will begin to watch you to see if you fail or succeed. Your perseverance might be the catalyst needed to inspire your loved ones to be healthy.

"Our chief want is someone who will inspire us to be what we know we can be."

~ Ralph Waldo Emerson

VI.

I will no longer allow the opinions of others to cause me excessive stress and harm.

I have a confession. I used to be one of those people who felt that health only involves eating right and exercising, but a health scare early in my twenties proved how erroneous my thinking was. Living a healthy life also includes managing my stress levels properly. A large portion of my stress was attributable to drama from various relationships.

Stress is one of the leading contributors to many diseases, and often death. Opinions are like belly buttons, everyone has one, so listen to them with a discerning ear, and stay on your course.

"Someone's opinion of you does not have to become your reality."

~ Les Brown

VII.

The only fitness program I can fail is the one I never begin.

We all fall short of our goals at times. Don't use imperfection as an excuse to quit trying to get healthy. If you get off course, re-focus and get right back to the objective at hand.

"When the world says "Give up," Hope whispers "Try it one more time."

~ Author unknown

VIII.

I will no longer seek comfort in my inferiority complex.

Although we may not care to admit it, many of us find solace in mentally abusing ourselves. If you constantly remind yourself that you're not good enough, then you won't have to worry about taking on new challenges that you fear.

> *"It is a wretched taste to be gratified with mediocrity when the excellent lies before us."*
>
> *~ Isaac Disraeli*

IX.

*I will give my body the time
it needs to adjust to a new
healthier lifestyle.*

Changing long-term habits is one of the most difficult tasks that you can take on. Be kind to your body by allowing it to slowly adjust to healthy eating and exercise.

"Success is the sum of small efforts, repeated day in and day out."

~ Robert Collier

X.

I am not responsible for anyone else's failure or for their success.

We cannot carry people's burdens for them, nor should we. One of the gifts that we can give to our loved ones is to let them learn their own lessons, as we struggle to learn ours. This is the only way to find true wisdom.

"Accept responsibility for your life. Know that it is you who will get you where you want to go, no one else."

~ Les Brown

XI.

I will clear my mind of contaminated and chaotic thoughts that destroy my potential.

A healthy mind cannot create chaos. It only knows how to work toward productive thinking and behaviors.

"In a disordered mind, as in a disordered body, soundness of Health is impossible."

~ Cicero

XII.

I am a beacon of light to guide the paths of others.

Do you find yourself constantly trying to save everyone and consequently end up on the losing end? Don't underestimate the power of your example. You never know whom you may inspire from day to day. Find the courage to shine so that you might light the path for someone else.

"And as we let our own light shine, we unconsciously give other people permission to do the same. As we're liberated from our own fear, our presence automatically liberates others"

~ Marianne Williamson
("A return to love")

XIII.

I will not wait for a death sentence to begin my health journey.

We often take things for granted until we have to stare the consequences in the face. For example, how many people would continue to abuse their bodies if they knew that they had a limited time to live?

"To think too long about doing a thing often becomes its undoing."

~ Eva Young

XIV.

*I deserve to wake up each
and every morning loving me,
as I am!*

Stop apologizing for the joy and success in your life. You were created to be a winner! Adorn yourself with love and positivity and keep moving forward through every obstacle.

"No one can make you feel inferior without your consent."

~ Eleanor Roosevelt

XV.

I am a beautiful and amazing example of Nature's glory, and I radiate goodness.

Through enriching your body with natural foods and drinks, you will emanate a healthy glow that is apparent to everyone who comes into contact with you.

"Take care of your body. It's the only place you have to live."

~ Jim Rohn

XVI.

I refuse to take part in the pity game any longer. Feelings of sorrow only delay happiness in my life.

Every morning you should rejoice that you are alive! Don't waste another moment focusing on what you don't have. Life is full of precious treasures when we open our eyes. Life is going to continue with or without you, so why not make the decision to be an active participant in your journey. Reminiscing about the unfairness that you've been dealt won't help anyone.

"A journey of a thousand miles begins with a single step"

~ Lao Tzu

XVII.

I am worthy of a healthy life and I deserve to live free of pain.

It is every person's unalienable right to live his/her best life. Illness and disease don't have to be handed down to you. You have the power within you to change your mind, your spirit, and your body.

"You yourself, as much as anyone in the entire universe deserve your love and affection."

~ Buddha

XVIII.

In order for me to lead my healthiest life, I cannot live someone else's life for them.

It's perfectly healthy to want to nurture and teach our loved ones, but it can be very dangerous to take on the responsibility for someone else's happiness. As we become healthier human beings, we also become better parents, friends, sisters, brothers, grandparents, and role models; and, therefore, we help create a foundation for a healthier community.

"Be the change you want to see in the world."

~ Mahatma Gandhi

XIX.

I will no longer confuse humility with self-deprecation. I don't have to put myself down to love others.

Humility is a beautiful trait that we should all aspire to have, but it is crucial not to confuse being humble with putting yourself down. You don't have to brag about your greatness, but never deny it either.

"Too many people overvalue what they are not, and undervalue what they are."

~ Malcolm S. Forbes

XX.

*I have a purpose in this life,
and I deserve the opportunity
to find it.*

Your life is waiting for you to begin living it. There is no other person on this earth who has the same destiny as you do, so bear down, focus, and dare to walk towards the life you've only dreamed.

"If one advances confidently in the direction of one's dreams, and endeavors to live the life which onc has imagined, one will meet with a success unexpected in common hours."

~ Henry David Thoreau

XXI.

*A healthy life begins with the
way I treat myself.*

If I can't be good to myself, how can I be a positive force in the life of anyone else?

"The way you treat yourself sets the standard for others."

-- Sonya Friedman

XXII.

Every day I will work toward
freeing myself of negative
thoughts and behaviors
that deter me from a living
healthy life.

Transformation begins with a single action that multiplies into many. Begin to live healthier by simply thinking positive thoughts.

"All negativity is an illusion created by the negative mind to protect and defend itself."

~ Ambika Wauters

XXIII.

I surround myself with mentally and spiritually healthy people, so that I am constantly aware of maintaining a positive outlook in all circumstances.

People can be the most powerful deterrent to the accomplishment of your goals. As an adult, it is your right and responsibility to surround yourself with people that will support your quest to become healthier.

"Happiness is an attitude. We either make ourselves miserable, or happy and strong. The amount of work is the same."

~ Francesca Reigler

XXIV.

By putting the needs of everyone before my own, I subconsciously tell my mind, body, and spirit that I don't matter.

Every one of the trillion cells in your body receives its orders from your brain. When you continuously engage in unhealthy behaviors, you are sending a message to these cells that says, "I don't value myself."

"My purpose on this earth is no greater and no less than anyone else's."

~ Basheerah Ahmad

XXV.

I refuse to complain about my physical condition, and I will take steps toward becoming healthier.

Constantly telling the world about your sickness or pain will not heal you. Instead, begin to speak wellness into your body and your mind.

"Instead of complaining that the rosebush is full of thorns, be happy that the thorn bush has roses."

~ Proverb

XXVI.

*I will no longer allow
excuses to paralyze my mind
and actions.*

Fear is a very real threat to the evolution of any person who cannot control it. We often fear that which is unfamiliar or unseen. Instead of facing this emotion, many of us come up with numerous excuses why we can't do something that we ought to. To become healthy, you have to step out of your comfort zone, face your fears, and have faith in the outcome of your new behaviors.

"Ninety-nine percent of the failures come from people who have the habit of making excuses."

~ George Washington Carver

XXVII.

*My primary motivation
is to live a healthier and
happier life.*

Be very clear about why you want to get healthier. Goals quickly lose the "wind in their sails" when your motivation is unknown.

"Obstacles are those frightful things you see when you take your eyes off your goal."

~ Henry Ford

XXVIII.

*During my weakest moments,
I am presented with an
opportunity to be renewed
with strength.*

It is at these precise moments that I may be fortunate enough to realize my greatness. Sometimes we must be broken down in order to be rebuilt in a healthier way. There is a great sense of power that comes with overcoming adversity.

"Success is to be measured not so much by the position that one has reached in life…as by the obstacles which he has overcome while trying to succeed."

~ Booker T. Washington

XXIX.

My mind and spirit receive constant nourishment from the things I choose to surround myself with.

Start to change your habits and surroundings. If you want to be in a healthier place mentally, spiritually, and physically then venture out to find more. Instead of watching soaps and reality TV when you get home from work, find a program on transformation. Or better yet, read a book or article about a topic you have interest in.

"If you nurture your mind, body, and spirit, your time will expand. You will gain a new perspective that will allow you to accomplish much more."

~ Brian Koslow

XXX.

When I feel that I lack the strength or discipline to move forward in my quest for health, I will stand still and be grateful for my simple existence.

When you become frustrated and overwhelmed, one of the worst things you can do is to give up. We all have moments where we feel inadequate and powerless. It is during these times that we have to sit still and be content just to "be."

"Silence is a source of great strength."

~ Lao Tzu

XXXI.

I release all feelings of shame, guilt, and inferiority that have led me toward self-destructive behavior.

Every day is a new opportunity to determine your path to happiness. As difficult as it may be, you have to let go of the past, and you have to release your feelings of ineptitude if you are ever to move forward.

"We must be willing to let go of the life we have planned, so as to accept the life that is waiting for us."

~ Joseph Campbell

XXXII.

I trust my body, and will listen as it tells me what I need in order to be healthy.

The human body is the most complex and intelligent machine ever created. Our bodies give us signals to help prevent sickness and disease. When we consciously choose to rid our bodies of toxins and numbing agents, then we are able to work toward rebuilding a channel of communication with ourselves.

"God created us with all the tools that we need to exist."

~ Basheerah Ahmad

XXXIII.

*My mental and physical health
is a priority in my life.*

My decision to get healthy is for me. I'm not doing it to please anyone or to prove a point. A healthier mind and body will give me a better quality of life.

"Health is a state of complete harmony in the body, mind, and spirit. When one is free from physical disabilities and mental distractions, the gates of the soul open."

~ BKS Iyengar

XXXIV.

*I will stop answering my
yearning to pursue my dreams
with a "no."*

We are often our own worst enemy. It's as if we all have a personal critic that picks and chooses the opportunities it feels best suit us. But, this critic is often the voice of insecurity and leads us to lack of fulfillment. Learn to silence this critic and follow your heart.

"Dreams are illustrations…from the book your soul is writing about you."

~ Marsha Norman

XXXV.

*I will no longer criticize
the actions and behaviors
of others.*

Love yourself enough to be healthy

When you pass judgment on the lives of others, you are truly revealing your own insecurities and fears.

"Any fool can criticize, condemn, and complain, but it takes character and self-control to be understanding and forgiving."

~ Dale Carnegie

XXXVI.

I will never love anyone or anything more than I love myself.

You may have a hard time accepting this affirmation, especially if you are woman. From early childhood, we have been brainwashed into believing that everyone should come before we do, and this is a lie. The truth is that we should love ourselves as we love our brothers, not less than. Isn't this the true essence of The Golden Rule?

"Love yourself first and everything else falls into line."

~ Lucille Ball

XXXVII.

I will love myself with every flaw, imperfection, and insecurity that I may have.

You were created from perfection! Embrace everything that you are, and focus your energy on being the best you possible.

"I don't like myself, I'm crazy about myself."

~ Mae West

XXXVIII.

I will acknowledge and reward myself for even small accomplishments. I am my biggest fan.

There is nothing wrong with being your own cheer captain. Don't wait on the praise and accolades from others, because it may never come, but even if it does, don't let it define your worth. You are amazing because you exist.

"Always be a first-rate version of yourself, instead of being a second-rate version of someone else."

~ Judy Garland

XXXIX.

Because of the love I have for myself, I will not participate in health-sabotaging activity.

When I participate in harmful activity, such as overeating, excessive drinking, or smoking, I send the wrong message to my mind and body.

"Without health, life is not life; it is only a state of languor and suffering—an image of death."

~ Buddha

XL.

I give myself permission to live a life not approved of by mainstream society.

You only get one shot at life. Don't waste it worrying about whether or not you are living up to the ever-changing standards of others. Live as if you only had to answer to the Creator.

"The individual has always had to struggle to keep from being overwhelmed by the tribe. To be your own man is a hard business. If you try it, you'll be lonely often, and sometimes frightened. But no price is too high to pay for the privilege of owning yourself."

~ Arthur Gordon

XLI.

I open up a channel of positive energy by embracing the success of others.

You should be as excited for someone else as you are for yourself. Sometimes life shows you your path through the lives of others.

"One man cannot hold another man down in the ditch without remaining down in the ditch with him."

~ Booker T. Washington

XLII.

I will never allow another human being to step on my dreams again!

People often underestimate the power of a healthy spirit. With clarity and vision comes a remarkable strength that will help you accomplish dreams unfathomable.

"Listen to your heart above all other voices."

~ Marta Kagan

XLIII.

I refuse to take shortcuts with harmful drugs, stimulants, and fad diets.

Because of the love I have for myself I will not put my health in jeopardy. Quick fixes are not lasting, and I want to learn how to live healthy for a lifetime.

"There are no shortcuts to any place worth going."

~ Beverly Sills

XLIV.

*Health is a destination that
I will pursue my entire life.*

No person has the perfect formula for overall health. Many people have healthy bodies but lack mental and emotional stability; and the same applies conversely. Becoming healthier involves learning how to balance all aspects of your life as you progress on your journey.

"A journey towards perfection leaves no room for the unexpected lessons that life can give us"

~ Basheerah Ahmad

XLV.

I reject all self-loathing and self-critical ideas that keep me from accomplishing my health goals.

When will you give yourself permission to be healthy, and ultimately free? Any negative idea or opinion that comes from your mind can be substituted with a positive one.

"A pessimist sees the difficulty in every opportunity; an optimist sees the opportunity in every difficulty."

~ Winston Churchill

XLVI.

*As I love myself healthier,
my capacity to love others is
also increased.*

Self- love is contagious. When you truly love who you are, then you have no choice but to love your fellow man, who is your mirror image.

"You shall love your neighbor as yourself."

~ Matthew 22: 37-40

XLVII.

Every cell in my body is
renewed with life and vitality.

Health begins on a cellular level. As we feed our bodies wholesome foods, our cells begin to regenerate, and become better equipped to fight disease and parasites. Consistent exercise can also regenerate brain cells as well as muscles and organs.

"The very foundation of our core existence is rooted in natural health."

~ Basheerah Ahmad

XLVIII.

A positive attitude in a healthy body can be the spark to ignite powerful change.

The world is truly your oyster when you give yourself a fair shot at happiness.

"Clear your mind of toxic thoughts and clear your body of toxic waste, so that you can operate from a position of clarity."

~ Basheerah Ahmad

XLIX.

I forgive myself for not being more than I am.

Blame and ego can be poisonous elements to the human mind, body, and spirit. Be proud that you are perfectly imperfect, and dare to live your best life!

"Striving for excellence motivates you; striving for perfection is demoralizing."

~ Harriet Braiker

L.

Failure and Rejection will no longer cripple my advancement in life.

How will you know how strong you can be if you are never tested? Winning was never supposed to be easy, just well worth the effort.

"Every adversity has within it the seed of an equivalent or a greater benefit."

~ Napoleon Hill (Grow Rich with Peace of Mind)

18796719R00063